For Ora Mae Kirk and Dr. Jan Haluska.

THIS ONE LONG PROMISE

Poems

David L. Denton

CONTENTS

The Warrior...1
The Heart Chooses...2
The Wedding Ring..3
Traveler...5
Unspoken..6
Dreams...7
Too Soon...8
The Healer..9
Fathoms 10
Anatomy Lesson...11
A Fly Inspiration..12
A Foreign Policy...13
After All is Said and Done...14
After the Funeral 15
Inadequate 16
One Day 17
Gold...18
A Hand to Hold 19
Anniversary 20
Hide and Seek 21
Home Body 22
Between the Lines...23
What I Could Do...24
Insomnia...25
For All I Know 26
This One Long Promise 27
Birthday Wishes...28
Memories..29

For J.E.D. (The Reunion) 30

Mysterium 31

By the Side of the Road 32

Playing Pretend 33

Cautionary 34

Slippage 35

The Artist 36

First Love 37

The Awakening 38

The Beginning 39

Cloudland Canyon 40

Cold Comfort 41

Desire (Shiny Things) 42

The Patient 43

The Sacrifice 44

Discovery 45

Fair Warning 46

The Squirrel 47

Dreams 48

The Trinket 49

Ellipses 50

Estate Sale 51

Lover's Lament 52

The First Lesson 53

The Soldier Poet 54

Snatch-Away 55

The Prodigal 56

memoriam in absentia 57

The Drought 58

The Gift 59

Making the Best of Things 60

November 3 61

The Last to Know 62

Shadows 63

Process 64

Ghost Train 65

True Colors 66

The Visitation 67

Homecoming 68

New Mother 69

The Substance of Things 70

Sundown 71

On the Wheel 72

The Quest 73

At Bedtime 74

Old Friend (Wishful Thinking) 75

In the Moment 76

For All I Know 77

The Road to Hell 78

Self-Control 79

The Sympathizer 80

Loss 81

The Forecast 82

The Veteran 83

Short Pier 84

Blind, Leading 85

The Worship 86

On Opening Our Eyes 87

The Invitation 88

The Critic 89

The Warrior

Don't want a battle, didn't ask to fight,
But load the torpedoes and line the sight.
Marshal the forces and draw up the plans,
Knowing the outcome is out of my hands.
Turn into the wind and spit with a curse,
And dare the enemy to do his worst—
It's what makes us human, proves we're alive,
To fight on knowing we may not survive.
Ah, damn the torpedoes homing on me,
And damn all the radicals roaming free.
Like France in the war, I'm forced to retreat,
But I will not yield; I'll fight street by street.
I've allies beside me, weapons untried;
I will remain undefeated inside.

The Heart Chooses

Elijah, offered money for his cure,
Declined in honest effort to be pure
In both his healing action and intent,
And though entreated he remained unbent.

The victim, healed, departed for his land,
And took with him a bit of holy sand
To worship on and claim a stake for God.
And glancing back, he must have thought it odd--

The servant of the healer coming fast
To ask the share of gold his master passed.
We should not judge too harshly this deceit
Or lay the guilt too quickly at his feet.

Never mind how harshly guilt accuses,
The heart chooses what the mind refuses.

The Wedding Ring

I finally found your ring--
The one I thought was lost when I lost you.
That was too much loss for me.
Loss on top of loss, piling high
Until I thought I'd suffocate from the weight.
Every breath an exercise of will
And pain.

But I found the ring at last.
Or daddy did. "Over there," he pointed--
Couldn't even move himself
To get it for me. His own grief.
Perhaps, paralyzes. I should
Understand, I know; you'd want me to. Always
You'd preach patience. How I crave your words
Again—

Futilely, for you are gone.
And what do I have left? A few papers?
Some mementos? Memories?
God! The memories, piling high,
Waiting for me to find courage to sort them
Out, reminding me of every place
We've been.

Begin with this ring I found--
Your wedding ring I wear on my finger.

Now, because I can't hold you—
And work backward from there.
This ring foreshadowed me and constrained your life.
I wear it for the Love I felt but can't
Explain.

Traveler

So you're a traveler now, on your own road,
Far nearer the beginning than the end.
Unweighted yet by life's accreted load.
You still see adventure around each bend.
The toll the travel takes will tell the tale
In time but, eyes with wonder wide, you search
Around yourself as if the Holy Grail
Awaited your arrival in the Church
Of Always Moving Forward. It may be
Truth to which you travel, but there are side
Trips to entice, points of interest to see.
Still, you're no tourist here. You may decide
Someday you've seen enough, to your surprise,
And there you'll end your trip and rest your eyes.

You whispered something that I didn't hear,
So I asked you to repeat, leaning near.
But you demurred and, smiling, turned your head,
To leave me only ghosts of words you said.
Not the first time, and not the last, I fear.
Sometimes the spirit may be all we need,
If we can see beneath the words we read,
Or hear between the words what we intend.
What is it that we feel we must defend,
And who will heal the hearts that words make bleed?

You say you've nothing worthwhile to impart,
But you write love in every empty space.
I hear the music playing in your heart.
And see life's lyric written on your face.

Last night I dreamed a dream, no wonder there:
I've surely dreamt of more than I'm aware.
Had night visions I couldn't understand—
Somber missives from my soul's desert land.
Sometimes I'll wake up with a memory
Of having dreamed a dream that's gone from me.
And I've no Daniel who can come reveal
The meanings or the dreams the nights will steal.
Perhaps all dreams forgotten are the same
Dream repeated, and it is to my shame
That I can't hear the call of my own heart
Over the sound of life falling apart.
To sleep, perchance to dream, the Poet said:
I'd settle for a dreamless sleep instead.

Too Soon

I swear I hear you calling me sometimes,
But that is foolishness I know, just my
Imagination, just wishful thinking.
I should let go; I promise I will try.
I know that you'd rest better if I did.
But it feels like betrayal all the same,
Like I let go of you too easily--
Your picture's gone, all that's left's the frame.
You would say, "Don't worry about your heart."
You'd say you always knew my heart was true.
But can you see from where you are I'm lost,
As absent from this broken world as you?
You may live on entirely in my mind;
But that at least's a world of my design.

The Healer

I've brought to you this bird I found today,
Because I know your heart will find a way
To restore him (Or her--how does one know?)
Into the path of life a bird should go.
A sigh. "But I'm no expert," you protest.
I don't reply; your heart will do the rest
Of the convincing--do my work for me.
Is what you would say. You were called to be
A holder of birds--broken, small, afraid,
Cowering in the cradle your love made
Of your two hands. No expert? Yes, I know.
But love ventures where expertise can't go.
This bird is not the only life I've brought
To you to save, to heal what I could not.

Fathoms

This vastness overwhelms me as I sail
From here to You. Clouds are not companions,
And waves provide no comfort when I fail.
There is this mocking water bird that runs
Just out of reach, so I guess there is land
Just out of sight, as You seemed pleased to be.
They say You spoke, or maybe moved Your hand,
And life appeared--but not that I can see.
Across this flat and featureless seascape,
No life appears or speaks up from below.
Sometimes I fear there will be no escape
Into Faith from the emptiness I know.
Whatever meaning may below me be,
I sail here, on the surface of the sea.

Anatomy Lesson

Your heart is in your hands in the same way
The soul of any bird is in its song.
I know you've heard them, and you call to them
With desire far too lovely to be wrong.
They sing their songs for you; you're sure of this,
The same way you are sure of me. Some things,
You breathe in silent prayer, must simply be.
Or what could ease the pain of sorrows sting?
Just now a sassy sparrow's marked you out
As muse, your window his theater screen.
You have no words, just your hand at your mouth,
But you feel sure the bird knows what you mean.
Just as I do—your hands contain your heart;
I watch them dance each time the birds' songs start.

A Fly Inspiration

A desperate fly buzzing at my window
Saw a world outside where he could not go.
He was not restrained for lack of trying,
Though he could not see what was denying
Him his chosen path. He seemed to forget
What he had learned each time, his mind was set
So blindly on his goal. He tried again
And again, as if will alone could win
A battle that he could not understand.
I thought if I could catch him in my hand,
I'd intervene and set him free outside.
I made a vow that I would not decide
To settle for what logic says is true,
But learn by trying what I cannot do.

When did it all turn into only words?
Would we be better off if we used swords
Instead? There's too much passion here to speak,
And words won't bring the victory we seek.
We should have known words wouldn't be enough.
Victories are won with weapons in hand.
Armor, ammunition, a battle plan.
Even the poet, David, with his sling
Did not trust mere words to inflict the sting
That would be felt by nations through the rough
And bloody battlefields down through the years.
Yet here we are reciting ancient fears
And ancient claims of this or that wrong done,
Expecting words will make our giants run.

After All is Said and Done

After all is said and done, do not praise
Extravagantly what you cannot know.
Do not fling flowers, do not mourn the days
You think you've lost with me. I could not show
You how much of life was Show; I meant well,
Meant to stand upright even when I fell.

I meant to love you selflessly and strong,
And learned too late I did not have the heart.
I had the best intentions all along,
And learned that good intentions fall apart.
No eloquence required at the end,
I'm learning what it's like to not pretend.

One truth rings through until the final call:
I could have loved you better after all.

After the Funeral

They say goodbye or they don't
You say you'll be fine, but you won't
In the end it's always the same,
And words never ease the pain.
You tell yourself to move on,
Let go, the others have gone.
But there's a reason you stay around here
Making love to the hurt that you fear
And there's a reason I stay here with you.
Endure the same hurt that you do:
It's something to do with our heart
And at least we can say it's a start

Inadequate

Almost, not quite, just possible goodbyes,
Somehow always call real tears to my eyes.
All this pain, anticipating sorrow
Sure to come on some sad tomorrow,
Promises no peace for me, nor comfort,
Nor healing for good friends we know who hurt.
It's not time yet, they say, to shed a tear-
No tears to cry to make a difference here.
But still they come, still uselessly they come,
Until my face has, like my heart, grown numb.
I always thought you hung that silver moon;
You shone on me, my sun at highest noon,
I weep for you, and for this truth I know--
I can't be brave enough for my hero.

One Day

And this, also, is true
I've nothing to offer worthy of you
To comfort you
One day, here or somewhere,
A comfortable couple will talk and share
In peace we'll share
Our dreams and sorrows
And all our visions of bright tomorrows
Long tomorrows
For one day only we
Will like children pretend that we are free
And love is free
And we'll speak of heroes
Our mothers and missed love and how life goes
On, how it goes
One day only we'll walk
Together forever and we will talk
Our hearts will talk

Gold

There is gold in these hills, the miners say,
And they swear they will dig it out someday.
Every now and then a vein is found
And desperate dreamers swarm from miles around
To stake their claim and try to make it pay.

They always seem to leave a saddened lot,
Burdened more by dreams than the gold they sought.
I'm no prospector, but I have a sense
Their fruitless search, no matter how intense,
Was doomed to fail because their dreams were caught

Envisioning an artificial gold;
A gold good only to be bought and sold.
The gold these hills contain lies plain as day,
Not in but on the land where sunbeams play.

A Hand to Hold

Here's a hand (all I have to give) to hold:
Hold it with your hand and heart. Are you cold?
I've a blanket; and I can cover you
With all of me. And you know I would, too!
I'd lay right out and never let you go.
There's a secret truth both of us know,
Though we have never said the words aloud--
You from kindness; me? Perhaps I'm proud.
I pretend I am being strong for you,
Brave in the face of all you're going through,
To give you strength to face the truth you fear.
But I have never been the strong one here.
It's not my strength that keeps me holding you;
I'm far too weak to know else to do.

Anniversary

So this is the day that everything changed,
My heart and my soul became rearranged,
This is the day that you told me would come;
You didn't tell me it would leave me so numb.
You didn't tell me for how could you know
The fear I would feel but could not let show?
For all of the things we shared unrestrained,
Mother and daughter, this one truth remained--
I could not go yet, and you could not stay,
So we could not share the truth of this day.
You gave me the courage you had to give,
And out of my loss I learn how to live.
This is the day, and it will be again,
Year after year, till I follow you in.

Hide and Seek

There you are, you said, and smiled a smile
That told me you'd been looking for awhile.
But you were glad to find me, I could tell,
And I was tired of hiding, just as well.
It wasn't the first time we'd played this game.
But it felt new and dangerous just the same.
Nor has it always been a game. I know
You know, and we have secrets yet to show.
If I seemed shocked you found me, understand:
This is a new and undiscovered land.
Nobody's ever searched so hard before,
Content to tap once lightly on my door.
I've been found, and become a finder, too:
For I'd spent my whole life looking for you.

Home Body

We finally took that trip we'd always planned,
The one that you would annually demand,
Playfully, while we calculated bills,
Expenses, and the cost of cheaper thrills,
And then delayed, acknowledging the truth
Of too little money. The dreams of youth,
So tinged with tragedy we clearly see
Only when our eyes lose their clarity,
Remain our blanket and our unmade bed,
The table where lies our wine and bread.
We recall pleasant dreams, our might-have-beens,
And this one dream we lived. When this trip ends,
I will be glad, for all the sights we've seen
To just be at home with ourselves again.

Between the Lines

We never said goodbye that I recall.
In our separations it was all
That we could do to simply smile through tears.
And wear a face too brave to admit fears.
We said so long. see you later. take care.
We gave. "I love you", as a suit to wear.
We touched as if the touch would see us through;
And when you slid from me and I from you,
We owned the joyful hope of a return.
When once again the fire of love would burn.
There's no return tonight. we know. my love:
The power in our words is not enough.
And so we settle for the truest lie.
And say. "I love you." when we mean goodbye.

What I Could Do

All I have to offer is a poem—rhymes
And rhythm, communicating . . . What? Love?
Sorrow? Sadness? Empathy? There are times
We long for some expression from above,
Some rainbow promise of never again
To cool us from this hell that we are in.

What if Heaven has no voice but these lines,
No courage but what's in another's heart?
All I can offer are these word designs
And what cold comfort empty words impart.
I'd reach across this vastness if I could,
To save you from your own heart-sinking flood.

But you know, as do I, the gulf's too great,
And even Heaven's help arrives too late.

Insomnia

I wake most every morning, 3:00 a.m.,
As remnants of some darktime dream grow dim.
Unfinished business from the day before
Intrudes upon my rest, demanding more.
No polite hello or how do you do,
No excuse me if I'm disturbing you;
A sudden jerk, and there I am awake,
Trying not to move for my lover's sake.
She needs her sleep, God knows, and so do I,
And I'll not be the one who will deny
The sweet reward of rest that she has earned.
This is, at least, one lesson I have learned
And also: though we may share everything,
One should not share a rude awakening.

For All I Know

The me you fell in love with disappeared,
Vanished in a slow decay years ago,
And left you grasping at the emptiness
I left behind, vainly. For all I know,
You're still a true believer in my heart,
In some inherent goodness that you saw.
For all I know, you've stored away some piece
Of me, some sliver of my soul to draw
Into the light and smile, remembering.
You keep that remnant safe for me, you hear?
There must be value there I didn't see
(As you have learned, my vision isn't clear).
Perhaps some hidden gold, for all I know;
A part of me that broke off long ago.

This One Long Promise

There will be promises today, spoken
From full hearts before family and friends.
Long promises, they will be, and deep vows,
To carry you together through the ends

That come, must surely come, for all things cease
In time. Freshness stales, passion pales, shoes black
With perfect polish scuff and fade. All things
Yield to the tyranny of time, fall back

From whatever heights they have risen to
In honor of this moment when Life lives
Anew. All things end except for this one
Long promise that perpetually gives

A place for love imperfect to renew
And find a sheltered place in each of you.

Birthday Wishes

Do not confuse the joy that I express;
For though it's true I cannot love you less
It's also true I cannot love you more--
On your island, protected by your shore.

For every day's a day of birth and death.
Some take their first and some take their last breath.
And some will breathe inconsequential air,
Leaving no mark, no reason we should care.

They flash and flutter, flicker in the flame,
On this hurtling earth you were sent to tame.
Perhaps I loved your heart, but had no claim;
It would have been enough to know your name.

You celebrate the Earth gone round again;
I savor grace that gave you as my friend.

Memories

We hold on tightly to our memories
For memories are all we truly own.
All else is borrowed, temporary, frail,
A truth we fear; a fear we've always known.
I held your hand, and once I caught your eye,
Reflected in the sun--one day we seized
Of thousands we have had and then let go,
Hoping with this one we could both be pleased.
One? Or thousands? No difference at all,
For there is nothing truly ours to keep
Except the moments that my mind maintains,
Eternal, ephemeral, treasured deep
Inside a heart when all else turns to rust.
We hoard our memories because we must.

For J.E.D. (The Reunion)

To meet again, after the time we passed
Apart—did it seem long to you? To see
Your face give up an unsure smile for me
As I remembered how we parted last.
Not friends—no, never friends—and sister seems
As out of place as friend. Perhaps we thought
We wouldn't bear the scars of battles fought,
These wars of words we carried to extremes.
Perhaps we thought that nothing stays the same,
And so our hurting hearts had healed somehow.
But in your fleeting smile I saw just now
A flash of fear that vanished as it came.
A fear that we were what we were before
And I had only learned to hate you more.

Mysterium

We wonder why we are and what we've done
In teasing conversations on the run.
Fruitless Freuds, though amateurs, we pursue
Meaning and intent, as if those are true
Markers of what matters. I cannot say
Why I go this and not another way,
Or why I smile to cover up a tear.
I cannot say what I am doing here,
Or you--what Vision keeps you here with me?
I'd understand goodbye, you know I would,
And understand you did the best you could;
Your meaning, your intent, were clear to me--
No one's to blame for what could never be.
No sorrow here, no guilt, no wasted day;
There's nothing you could do here anyway.

By the Side of the Road

I was going somewhere but lost my way,
So I pretend I'm waiting for another day.
Don't mind these weeds grown all around;
I'm more than just another lost car you have found.
Don't mind these windows, empty gaping holes
Venting the spirits of the human souls
That once rode with me on time's highway.
Note the direction I face where I rest,
Into the sun setting red in the west.
I had a dream, a destination in mind;
Though I couldn't be sure what exactly I'd find.
I didn't anticipate the stop on the way,
Or think it was more than an hour's delay.
A spark plug gone bad? Or something more cruel?
Wait for the man to return with some fuel?
I forget what it was--time has a way--
But here's where I stopped, and here's where I stay.
I've seen others go by in a hurry somewhere,
And I try not to mourn that I will never get there.
This is what happens, do you understand?
Everything yields to ennui's demand.
Shiny grows dull, ambition grows tame,
What's new will grow old, and the earth will reclaim.

Playing Pretend

Born out of time, else I'd have been a knight,
Brave defender of all that's good and right.
See me in my armor, my chain and mail;
Upon my sturdy steed, I shall not fail
To battle through the Darkness to the Light!
And you my damsel in distress may be,
Chained up in your castle; I'll set you free.
I'll fight the fearsome dragon unafraid,
And find the gold wherever it's been laid.
This dream remains, this childhood fantasy,
I could fight for truth in some other world,
Whilst chaotic evil around me swirled.
I can't undream this noble knight I'd be,
But I don't know how to save you from me.

Cautionary

It's not the Before when passion first blooms,
It's not the anticipation that dooms
The heart or mind to relentless regret,
As memory does its best to forget.
It's not the During, when action is sweet,
And blood is pounding a passionate beat.
It's not the moment when reason dissolves
That true understanding finally evolves.
The moment of truth, bringing light and pain,
Will often shine brightest after the rain,
Reflecting in puddles bright on the ground
And washing away any pleasure found.
Before and During we do what we choose--
The After comes after, demanding dues

Slippage

The water in my hand was cold, so cold,
And though I tried my best I could not hold
More than just the tiniest residue.
And it seems that's all I have left of you.
I dipped my hand again and closed it tight,
And closed my eyes as well against the sight
As if what I could not see was not real.
But even with my eyes closed I could feel
Escaping water slipping from my hold
The way your face is fading from my soul.
I was a child; I'm not a child today.
But I still cling to things that fade away.
I could not hold water; I can't hold you;
I can't keep my heart from breaking in two.

The Artist

The way your face fell open at the sound
Of your song playing; the way the rhythm
Resonated with your soul, moved around
Inside your spirit--and you danced with them,
The players, I mean, who seemed to know your heart.
The tragic dance you always danced alone,
For no one else would hear the music start,
Is still the sweetest moment that you've known.
Perhaps you're still looking for one who hears
Beneath the music like you do? The loss
You lived for all those lonely years, the fears
You sang to sleep each night at any cost--
Oh, you were the music; you were the words,
But nobody played you, nobody heard.

First Love

What was that look you gave me, casting eyes
Aside demurely when I glanced your way?
So much can be decided by a word,
Some accidental phrase we can't unsay.

See how the moon a silent witness keeps,
Remorseless sentinel of all our nights
And all my easy promises to you--
Though I meant every word, by heaven's lights.

Of course I did--an easy thing to do.
I swore, and crossed my heart, and hoped to die,
And said the things that hopeful lovers say.
Perhaps I'll find forgiveness by and by.

No less than human in my good intent,
We promise first and then ask what we meant.

The Awakening

So many things I would have changed
If I could, maybe rearranged
A little here, a little there.
I guess it's true life doesn't care
What we want, or don't. Lying here
Swaddled in my deathbed fear,

I still feel hurt I can't forget
And mourn what hasn't happened yet.
You stand beside my bed in tears,
And whisper love into my ears.
My hand in yours, a simple touch,
Your lover's heart I hurt too much,

Your angel voice soothes soft and low,
The only certain thing I know.
In the blindness of eyes closed tight
I see that there's another Light
That's shining on, around, within,
These walls, these floors, the hearts of men.

You do not see it, do you, love?
And yet you feel it real enough
To take my faithless hand in yours
And whisper low of different shores.
The Light you lived I finally see--
It changed the way you looked at me.

The Beginning

I asked you to let me in, and you did.
And once inside your heart I found my place
To rest, be safe, and live, and there I hid
And gloried in the beauty of your face,
And of memories that life cannot erase.
I wonder at how memories endure
Beyond their birthing moment to become
The accumulated stories of her
And him, you, me...us. Of course, we'll find some
Fault with memory's details as they come.
But the essence! The essence must be true--
That you believed in me, and I in you.
However memory tells our story's end,
It always starts with this--you let me in.

Cloudland Canyon

Sunlight falls unharmed down this mountainside,
Grasping handless, but not to check its slide.
Instead to wrap the clinging trees in light
Descending and anticipating night.

As a young child I dared the night to come,
Chased fireflies and heard the crickets' thrum
Until my mother called me from the door
And I returned, brave pirate to the shore.

And she would wrap her clinging son in love
And lay him down to sleep secure enough
To trust the night would pass, the light return—
The most important lesson one can learn.

I listen for a call as night descends
And long for a safe place as this day ends.

Cold Comfort

At least she's at peace, he said to his God,
And to himself, never thinking how odd
It might sound to the dead if the dead could
Still hear. They can't, nor can they feel peace. Should
We recognize that or honor the lie?
Would it be too cruel for us to deny
The mourner the momentary release
Of thinking their loved one's finally at peace?
Peace requires presence, and presence needs breath,
And nothing that matters is present in death.
The living need peace and take from the dead
What comfort they can to cover their dread
Of the deep stillness that passes for peace,
And of that dark time when memories cease.

Desire (Shiny Things)

I liked the shiny thing and took my chance
To add it to the things that I possess.
And other shiny things had me entranced;
Each new thing meant I loved the old things less.
Desperate to hold on to my desire
(For desire was the one sure thing I knew),
I built this room out of the blackest mire
For me to dump my shiny things into.
Outside the room I found I could not see
All the shiny things that I had locked away.
I made myself a space where I could be
At home here with my things, and here I stay.
Were I not living proof, I'd not have known
Desire can be a prison all its own.

The Patient

So many wounds accumulated here.
Unhealed and unhealable I fear.
Have scarred my heart and soul, and, through me, you.
I'd make amends if I knew what to do.
It's not enough to offer up regret.
Or hope that love will gracefully forget.
Never enough, no matter what I try.
I treat truth that hurts with a morphine lie.
So many drugs available to use
For so much hurt, I find I can't refuse
Whatever's offered to provide relief
And ease me from this pain beyond belief.
My drug of choice? A friend forever true:
But I can't medicate myself with you.

The Sacrifice

Oh, the wine and the bread, Sacrifice said,
Has healed the hearts of the doomed and the dead.
The blood and the body, spilled and broken,
The truest "I love you" ever spoken.
When Sacrifice served the supper that night
And knelt to wash feet he had made, the sight
Amazed, dismayed, and a pure love conveyed
To the men whose sin-debt would be paid.
From the room and the light, into the night,
To the garden to prepare for the fight.
His friends who were there were hardly aware,
Of the struggle they weren't able to share.
Selfishness said that there's Life in our pride;
Sacrifice died because Selfishness lied,

Discovery

I found those diverged roads the Poet said
Befuddled him and made it hard to choose
One over the other. The yellow wood.
Now white and black and bare so one could lose

One's self in the sameness, haunts me--taunts me--
With the invitation to choose. How much
Easier to settle here, not decide,
Until at last the beckoning woods encroach

And both roads disappear in brush and trees--
And I find myself rooted to this ground.
How easy . . . Yet impossible as well.
Two roads diverged, the only two I've found.

And one of them will carry me away.
And one of them will be my path someday.

Fair Warning

If you play with fire, son, you might get burned--
A lesson taught often, but not quite learned.
You can't be too careful, avoid the flame--
And now that I'm older, I say the same.
Funny what changes when the wheel has turned.

Don't play with fire, boy, and don't get too close.
Take it from me because I'm one who knows
What fire feels like when it's out of control.
There's a kind of flame that will burn your soul
Even if it never touches your clothes.

Don't play with fire--it seems so simple and clear,
The heat and the flames are easy to fear.
But what can you do and where can you go,
When fire is the only playmate you know?

The Squirrel

Today I saw a squirrel in perfect fright
Scramble here and there, imperfect flight
That left him, when he settled, still right there
And thinking to himself how life's not fair.
I can imagine as the car bore down
Relentlessly upon him that the sound
Would overwhelm his little squirrel ears
And be the worst of all his squirrel fears.
And as he, frozen, watch the car approaching
Did he spend his last moments reproaching
And regretting chances never taken?
Can a squirrel ever feel forsaken?
Whatever else a squirrel may feel, or not,
I hope he never felt the pain of Thought.

Dreams

Last night I dreamed a dream, no wonder there;
I've surely dreamt of more than I'm aware,
Had night visions I couldn't understand—
Somber missives from my soul's desert land?
Sometimes I'll wake up with a memory
Of having dreamed a dream that's gone from me
And I have no Daniel to come reveal
The meanings or the dreams the nights will steal.
Perhaps all dreams forgotten are the same
Dream repeated, and it is to my shame
That I can't hear the call of my own heart
Over the sound of life falling apart.
To sleep, perchance to dream, William said;
I'd settle for a dreamless sleep instead.

The Trinket

This is not your heart lying on the ground,
This broken plastic trinket that you found--
This heart that never beat with joy or pain,
Broken in two and washed with cleansing rain.
Your heart of flesh still beats inside your chest,
Through trial and triumph, without peace or rest.
Your Human heart still bleeds real blood, and red,
And keeps you living life among the dead.
Sometimes it's hard to choose between the two--
Plastic heart? Or the human heart in you?
Sometimes the difference can be hard to see,
When you offer both, or either one, to me.
I know the difference, even if you don't;
I'll choose the real heart, even if you won't.

We live in the ellipses after words
Where all the possibilities remain.
Ellipses that fill spaces between words
Where we can let imagination reign,
And set the spirit free that words constrain.

I wrote a poem for you that's mostly space,
With room for you to add your own design,
To make what I constructed your own place,
Until you gave me leave to make it mine
And filled in the ellipses with a sign

To let me know that I was welcome here.
We love in the ellipses of our hearts,
Beyond the boundaries of our faithless fear.
What words cannot convey silence imparts.

Estate Sale

"Come early," urges the sign by the road,
At the base of the hill lifting the house
Regal and proud above the countryside,
Like a baron to whom fealty is owed.
No royalty this, just an empty shell,
Forlorn and forsaken, bereft of life
And a reason to be. You go early
To see what it is they're trying to sell.
A table and chairs, some jewelry and gold—
What life accumulates, death leaves behind.
This was a home in a house on a hill,
Now it's a store where life's remnants are sold.
Come early, and learn a lesson forgot:
The building remains, but the home does not.

Lover's Lament

I cannot be anybody's lover;
The reservoir from which I'd draw is drained.
I've lived most of my life undercover;
Most of what I've called love is anger stained
With wishful thinking wrapped in self-deceit.
I'll give it my best shot, though, every chance
I get—hope springs eternal and all that,
But I don't expect I'll ever learn to dance
Or, to mix a metaphor, swing a bat
With any expectation of a hit.
I've tried to love, and want to love like you
Who make it seem an easy thing to do.
There's magic there, a rabbit from a hat,
A trick, illusion . . . something dumb like that.

The First Lesson

We came empty, drained from the long journey,
With gifts that seemed inadequate and small.
What gold or scented oil could satisfy
A King who is Creator of it all?

We came hopeful, witnesses to glory
Others somehow failed to see. Blinded eyes
Are often unaware that they are blind;
The Beauty they could see their heart denies.

We came desperate, across a desert of
Despair, hoping here we would find relief
From the incessant emptiness we knew
Encroaching on our fortress of belief.

We left as teachers; this is what we teach:
There are no children beyond this Child's reach.

The Soldier Poet

I would do battle if I had the means
To wage a war that I did not begin.
I was drafted, enlisted with no choice,
Into a conflict I can't hope to win.
Around me comrades fall, soldiers and friends,
And other casualties unnamed, unknown,
Forgotten here in memory's graveyard,
Beneath time's covering dirt without a stone.
I would do battle, not alone for me,
Nor yet for both of us and those we love,
But for the glory of the fight to live--
Though we both know I don't have strength enough,
And there's no chance that I'll cause fate to yield
When words are the only weapons I wield.

Snatch-Away

I played snatch-away with you every day,
It seemed, before you learned to walk or say
Your daddy's name. I would hold the toy--
It didn't matter which--this far away,
And you would reach laughing for the prize
I'd snatch away. After fruitless tries
Your laughter sometimes darkened to despair
As you learned (from me!) life can be unfair.
Still we played the game; I could not say why.
Always you would laugh; often you would cry
And look at me with disappointed gaze,
And at the toy, and then--was that a sigh?
Perhaps you caught a glimpse of how life goes,
And snatch-away's the only game life knows.

The Prodigal

I would have expected better weather,
More than a slivered sun, for my return.
Perhaps the poet in me is too strong,
And my teacher's soul still has more to learn
Of the vagaries of life. I belong
Here; Years and miles away I felt the tether
Constraining me and reeling me back in.
But...More sun, less gray—that's too much to ask?
It seems to me a fair enough request,
And I would think God equal to the task.
His people here on earth can do the rest
And celebrate me back from where I've been.
I'll not complain for all the miles I've come,
A short walk up this path and I'll be home.

memoriam in absentia

I'll never know the name engraved in stone
Above the plot I chose to bury you.
To know the name would mean I could not lie
And tell myself the metaphor is true.
I bury you in theory, not in fact,
And for that purpose this grave serves as well
As any other, the way perhaps my
Mother was a random choice for you. Hell,
They say, is separation from the Love
That ties us all together soul to soul;
My hell's that preemptive separation,
The father-son connection that you stole
(My birthright lost while I was in the womb)
And took with you into this borrowed tomb.

The Drought

Your dying grass drove you to near despair,
Browning beneath the blazing summer sun.
You raged against the poison in the air
Undoing all the gardening you had done.
A flower, newly wilted, caught your eye--
A rose, once bright and crimson, brought a tear,
As you knelt silently and sighed a sigh
That echoed forth a long unspoken fear.
A summer drought kills more than grass, you know,
And flowers aren't the only beauty lost.
We lose our souls across life's seasons, slow--
Too slow for us to measure out the cost.
When you regret the peace you never had,
Remember how the wrong things made you sad.

The Gift

The gift, unwrapped, made his lonely heart ache.
No ribbon or paper, no card or bow;
No box and no gift bag, nothing to shake.
A glance was enough for the man to know
The Gift-giver's love, the work of his hands,
Crafted uniquely with his joy in mind.
And there before him the Giver's gift stands,
Giver created and Giver designed,
Unmatched in beauty, unequaled in worth.
Search every store ever, you'll never find
Anything more perfect in all the earth.
Some gifts cost money--it's how the world goes;
The best gifts are made gifts, as Adam knows.

Making the Best of Things

If I lose my grip on the world I'm in,
And I cannot find my way back again,
I'll make a brand new world with room for two
And live life there alone except for you.
How we shall dance--I'll sing because I can;
In this other world I'm a better man.
Perhaps you humor me--your knowing smile
Sadly suggests dreams last a little while,
To be replaced by real life breaking in
Reminding us of heartbreaks where we've been.
No hearts would break in any world of mine;
Real life would yield before my grand design.
Oh! The world I'd make could I have my way,
And, oh, the joy--if only for a day.

You'd think three decades would have been enough,
But we're closing thirty years with no sign
The grieving ever will be gone for good
And I can find no meaning or design
In these opportunistic tears of mine

Expressing sadness I thought long suppressed.
As well to ask why rain falls when the sun
Shines, as to wonder why my heart still weeps,
Or why a mother loves a thankless son,
And loved him hard through all he left undone.

I know it's true that years can intervene,
But there are slates that cannot be wiped clean.
Though some hurts disappear beneath time's flow;
Regret's the longest sorrow that I know.

The Last to Know

I have seen this river peaceful, deep and
Calm, so that a face held over it would
Receive its own face back, framed mirror-like
By a background sky, by these unfettered trees.
I have heard this river singing, making
Music with the flutes of water eddied
In the branches laid on boulders that have
Defied the force of will this river brings
To bear. Perhaps I've known this waterway
Too well, become too close to know when I
Should fear. For though I hear its soft voice rise
In anger, and watch once languid water,
Frenzied, rush and swirl in violent alarm,
I disbelieve this friend would cause me harm.

Shadows

The first time I remember being scared
Was as a child discovering my twin,
My shadow, floating softly on the ground,
Connected to my body, end to end.
I ran in panic, trying to escape
And be myself again, alone and free.
I was not ready yet to be tied down
To something I'd not wanted that chose me.
Perhaps I've never grown beyond that child,
For there are shadows everywhere, I fear.
And they will find me if I stay too long
And that is why it's hard to keep me here.
So if I left too soon, I hope you see
It wasn't you I ran from, it was me.

Process

The sun is there, just where a sun should be,
Doing exactly what a sun should do.
The moon tonight, if clouds allow the view,
Will spray a spritz of silver down on me,
As I count all the lonely stars I see.

The world is turning, day to night to day--
The order of things, unchallenged, remains
In place, replete with all these myriad stains
Humanity has tried to rub away,
Converting what was black or white to gray.

Stay here with me another little while;
We'll wish upon the first star that we see.
There's order in the heavens, and a Guide,
And we are here still learning how to be.

Ghost Train

Some trains travel, touring transient towns,
Tracking time with a rhythmic steamy sigh.
Of hope? Or desperation? Who can say?
Some folks ride to come, some to get away,
But every train rides empty by and by.

Some trains travel, souls surfing seas of sound,
Secure against the wasteland passing by.
Until at last, some destination reached,
They wake to find their sanctuary breached,
And disembark into another lie.

And in this train this field claimed long ago,
How many lifetimes linger with a will
To finish what was started, for they know
That some trains travel farther standing still.

True Colors

The chameleon waited unsure of me,
Fearfully motionless, waiting to see
If I was a threat or could be ignored.

I wasn't sure if the color he showed
Was his color true or camouflage mode,
Designed to blend in 'til safety's restored.

And how could I tell, not knowing him well,
Which color he was when evening fell?
Is there one color that finally defines

A chameleon's essence so all can agree?
And what is my color--the truth of me?
The aura that shines through all my designs?

What am I really when colors all fade
Finally into one permanent shade?

The Visitation

(For JCH)

What a poor story these mementoes tell,
How insufficient as our memories swell,
How powerless our forlorn grief to quell,
Or bring to life what we remember well.
What picture frames the heart? Which of these plaques
Replaces what this broken vessel lacks?
Or how do we here, dressed in somber blacks,
In all our murmeration of your acts
Of beauty, spirit, of learning, of heart,
Resurrect the essence, of which a part
Is all we've really ever seen? The art
Of life is art beyond our dreams. We start
Anew each time we have to say goodbye,
To learn to love the Art that doesn't die.

Homecoming

I cannot tell you which one haunts me more,
The frozen truck or house missing its door.
I've entered by the door no longer there,
And ridden in that truck, oh, everywhere.

The echoes of a past I've long since lost
Remind me just how much my dreams have cost.
I can hear the ancient engine call me
One last time back home, if only to see

What has become of what I left behind.
Old friends, forgive me: offer me a sign
That life remains amidst this slow decay
To comfort me when I have lost my way.

These forlorn windows with their vacant stare
Are almost more than this lost son can bear.

New Mother

I saw your tear-streaked face look up at me
As if to ask how this much pain could be.
The crumpled sheets and antiseptic walls,
The ebb and flow of sorrow in the halls.
Contrasting with the new life promised here--
A counterpoint to everything we fear.
I saw your face, a helpless witness weak
Myself, and powerless as well to speak
Your pain away.

Remember all the rain.
The storm you thought had ruined our big day?
You don't, of course, just living moved us on.
This pain will go wherever that storm's gone,
Leaving behind this new life at your breast.
Embracing love, we lay aside the rest.

The Substance of Things

I have read between your lines,
Your conversational designs,
Heard unspoken pleas
For comfort and for peace.
I've seen your sun set and rise,
Reflecting sadly in your eyes,
Glory we cannot possess,
Light that shines on our distress.
Come talk with me and let me hear
The words you raise to hide your fear.
You're surprised, I know, that I
Understand what you deny
Even to yourself is real
(Whence comes this shame for what you feel?)
Oh, I can see inside so well,
How every heart hides its own hell,
How every smile covers a curse.
Because we know it could be worse.

Sundown

We thought the sky before us was the crown
Of glory, red rays reflecting the sun
Retiring, spilt across the span of sky
And speaking peace to our admiring eye.
Then you or I happened to glance around
To witness the sun itself going down
And understood the greater glory there,
The source of all the beauty in the air.
And as we drove in silence for awhile
The truth came clearer with each passing mile.
We live forward, dreams gleaming just ahead;
We rise with them and take them to our bed.
But now and then, pursuing them, we find
The greatest beauty haunts us from behind

On the Wheel

This long pursuit, of what I do not know,
Has kept me moving with no place to go.
I tell myself the movement is the thing
That validates the energy I bring
To bear upon my fruitless quest. I live
In motion while, directionless, I give
Direction, mindful of the irony
Of leading other people lost like me.
I shall keep faith until the bitter end,
Until the final curtain shall descend.
I shall pursue some end I cannot see,
Can never hold; some end that cannot be,
Till I discover, in the ground alone,
I am Sisyphus pushing up my stone.

The Quest

I've gone out searching for my Metaphor.
I've hung a "Be Back Soon" sign on my door:
In truth, though, I might not return at all.
I may be hearing an eternal call
That draws me ever outward till I fall
Into forever, soulless and unsure.

And if by chance you visit and you find
My door unanswered when you knock, be kind
And leave a memory or two for me,
Even though I can't tell you where I'll be,
Or when (if) I might return. Hope is free
Enough to offer even to the blind.

Tired of waiting for Meaning to appear,
I've gone searching the wasteland of my fear.

At Bedtime

It feels final falling into my bed,
Synapses switching off inside my head.
I've strength to fall, but not to rise again,
When morning comes with sunlight streaming in.
I can't say, "It is finished," for in truth
I fear I've barely started. In my youth
Such dreams and plans as you would not believe
Beguiled me with their power to deceive.
Another day has left me still bereft,
Uncertain of the time that I have left
To finish what I started years ago.
And if I succeeded, would I know?
It feels final like every night before,
And will until there's no night anymore.

Old Friend (Wishful Thinking)

These thirty years of could-have-been remind
Us both how quickly life can get away
(If wishes were horses, my mom would say),
And how certainty begins to decay
Into confusion. Are our lives designed
By outside forces beyond our control?
Or framed by every choice made unaware
Of any other path that might be there?
If I made a different choice, who would care?
Accumulated choice defines the soul,
Some say. I wonder if the opposite
Is true, and our souls measure, size, and fit
The choices that we make. I know what I'd
Choose—if our wishes were horses, we'd ride.

In the Moment

You can't survive your whole life in one day.
Some reserves, it seems, must be put away
Against some other time, another need.
No matter how our hearts may break or bleed,
We know that larger forces are at play,

And we may cauterize the wound with fire
Only to fall before some new desire
That leaps up—up, surrounding us with heat
Until we're drowned in the flames of defeat
We could not escape by climbing higher.

Perhaps the measure of how I survive
Is to be found in the effort I give
Within a moment. Can I say I live
If I survive one whole day in my life?

For All I Know

The me you fell in love with disappeared,
Vanished, in a slow decay years ago
And left you grasping at the emptiness
I left behind, vainly. For all I know,
You're still a true believer in my heart,
In some inherent goodness that you saw.
For all I know, you've stored away some piece
Of me, some sliver of my soul to draw
Into the light and smile, remembering.
You keep that remnant safe for me, you hear?
There must be value there I didn't see
(As you have learned, my vision isn't clear).
Perhaps some hidden gold, for all I know;
A part of me that broke off long ago.

The Road to Hell

The baby had intentions it was clear
To travel by some means from there to here.
But what his heart intended, legs declined
To honor. Reaching hands often would find
The floor, and he would sit down with a bump,
Wondering, I can't walk; how will I jump
Or run, or dance? Too much philosophy
For one so young. How soon we come to see
The gap between our plans and what we do.
Who among us doesn't want to be true?
Everybody talks--as if talk's the thing
(Knowing if talk mattered we'd all be King).
Myself? I know I'd set this world on fire
If my hands could fulfill my heart's desire.

Self-Control

Our sorrows are so solemnly expressed.
Our muted mourning masks a stormy heart
That lashes out against imposed constraints
And strains to tear Appropriate apart

We do not want to weep, but wail and rail
And rage against the loss of so much Good,
And shake our heads and raise our angry fists
And curse our loss until we plead the Blood.

But that's inside where it cannot be seen;
Where the world can see, we control our pain.
We treat as a virtue such self-control,
And hope we never face this fight again.

We're Christ in the Garden praying to be
Freed from the darkness of Gethsemane.

The Sympathizer

My sorrow's not for me for I've no loss;
I've not truly suffered, I've paid no cost
Of family separation, or lost to death
Too soon a son of my own flesh—my breath
Has not been spent in mourning my own child.

My sorrow is a common sadness shared
With you and with the soul this pain has bared.
If all that I can offer is this tear
That falls for you, I confess a lingering fear
That you will find my sympathy too mild.

But even though it may not be enough,
This tear that falls, falls from a well of love.
A well dug deep against this drought of sin;
A well from which I'll surely draw again.

Loss

This new day is too beautiful by far:
There is no hint of sadness where we are.
Here on the edge of the Pacific clouds
Surf the over-blue sky. But sorrow shrouds
Our vision and tears these moments mar.

The expanse of ocean eternally
Advancing and withdrawing seems to me
A cruelty, a mocking of our loss,
A reminder we are simply water tossed
In momentary wave crests on the sea.

Ah, God, I am not strong enough for this
Beauty or this pain. So I shake my fist
In pitiful defiance of a Sea
And Sky forever unaware of me.

The Forecast

You can see the storm coming miles away
Unless your back is turned and you refuse
To look. Still, anticipating trees sway
In rising wind gusts heralding the news,
And the dark horizon is a headline
Writ across this paper world. I have mine
Here safe with me--Safe? A moment's doubt.
Are we safer here within than without?
These walls that we have built were made to stand
Through any storm save those at God's command.
This isn't that, we tell ourselves and smile,
The world will carry on a little while.
I shiver in a sudden storm-brought chill;
The swaying trees grow ominously still

The Veteran

So he had scars, but not that you could see;
And she had dreams of what a man should be.
So dreams married scars; then the children came
Inheriting more than the family name.

Warriors learn through battles how to live,
And lovers learn through sacrifice to give:
But when the battlefield comes home, what then?
What can you give in battles no one wins?

The shrapnel scarred his skin, but not his heart;
The killing fields he won ripped him apart.
All the king's horses and all the queen's love
Would never, he would whisper, be enough—

He could not find the peace his spirit sought,
And all he knew was fighting, so he fought

Short Pier

Why don't you take a long walk, my sister
Said, off a short pier, and she turned away,
No doubt hoping, while her back was turned, that
I would have found some other place to play.

It was dismissal, probably deserved,
And I've been walking short piers ever since.
And it's been a long walk, too, I suppose,
But still I've never lost sight of the fence

Protecting me on either side. I know
There's a drop still waiting for me someday;
My sister's childhood wish will soon come true.
But I've always found a new place to play,

Friends to mourn even as their steps recede.
Life is a short pier, a short pier indeed.

Blind, Leading . . .

You forget the past
I forget the present
We both pretend the future
Is just a dream away
With your broken heart
You try to mend my soul
And blindness leading blindness
Leads both lost souls astray
We can't stop trying
Can we? We can't let what
Will be alone to be
We both reach darkly
Desperate, grasping, toward
A tomorrow we can't hold
Or even clearly
See

The Worship

I cannot tell you what these tears were for--
The hope I'd found? Or that I wasn't sure?
That, in spite of me, Someone showed me love?
Or fear that Someone's love is not enough?
Sitting by myself in church, three rows back,
And face to face with everything I lack,
Reminded of my weakness, in despair
I bowed my head in helpless, hopeful prayer.
And then the tears that I cannot explain
(In words that can communicate the pain)
Became holy in their baptizing flow
Reminding me of all I used to know.
I'm not alone, unless I choose to be;
I'm loved with Love more permanent than me.

On Opening Our Eyes

Stumbling awake a little bit post five,
I eye the clock, surprised I'm still alive.
I set a target time when I will rise,
Then sink back down and close protesting eyes,
Waiting for a good reason to arrive.

I will get up; I always have before.
I will get dressed; I will walk out the door
And face another day, to my chagrin;
A day unconcerned with the state I'm in,
And I'm unsure who hates the other more.

We've stopped all dialogue and now assert,
Oblivious to one another's hurt.
I will whine my whines, unconcerned with Day,
And Day, himself, has nothing good to say,
And so in silence I put on my shirt

And join the world, where I don't talk to you.
Either. Oh, Waking Up is hard to do!

The Invitation

You tried to pull me out onto the floor,
To mingle with the desperate bodies there.
You said I needed to let myself go,
Surrender to the passion in the air.
"I don't dance," I said, as I pulled away,
"I don't want to be humiliated
Pretending that I do." You looked at me
A moment, searching behind what I said
For the organic truth, and it occurred
To me that we all have skills we don't know.
I have learned to move to music no one
Hears but me, my own rhythm, my own flow.
I said I don't dance, but that is a lie.
Life is a ballroom: I'll dance 'til I die.

The Critic

There's a picture on a wall in a museum,
And people passing by will stop and stare
And wonder why the painting's hanging there
To confuse the unlearned when they come.

Full of implication and suggestion,
But lacking anything you'd recognize,
The picture is a torment for the eyes
(But not like staring too long at the sun).

They say minds can manufacture meaning,
And from foolishness can fashion Wisdom
Of a sort. Perhaps someday I will come
To appreciate what I'm demeaning.

Someday imagination will come back,
And fill the margins of the truth I lack.

Made in the USA
Columbia, SC
24 June 2023

18961647R00059